ALTERNATOR BOOKS™

THE UNOFFICIAL GUIDE

TO

MINECRAFT CONSTRUCTION

HEATHER E. SCHWARTZ

Lerner Publications ◆ Minneapolis

**A HUGE THANK-YOU TO NOLAN SCHWARTZ
AND EVAN BROOKS FOR PUTTING THEIR
SKILLS TO WORK CREATING SOME OF THE
PICTURES FOR THIS BOOK. YOU'RE AWESOME!**

Lerner Publications Company
A division of Lerner Publishing Group, Inc.
241 First Avenue North
Minneapolis, MN 55401 USA

For reading levels and more information, look up this title at www.lernerbooks.com.

Main body text set in Aptifer Slab LT Pro 11.5/18.
Typeface provided by Linotype AG.

Library of Congress Cataloging-in-Publication Data

Names: Schwartz, Heather E., author.
Title: The unofficial guide to Minecraft construction / Heather E. Schwartz.
Description: Minneapolis, MN, USA : Lerner Publishing Group, Inc., [2019] | Includes
    bibliographical references and index.
Identifiers: LCCN 2018012804 (print) | LCCN 2018023469 (ebook) | ISBN 9781541543515
    (eb pdf) | ISBN 9781541538849 (lb : alk. paper)
Subjects: LCSH: Minecraft (Game)
Classification: LCC GV1469.35.M535 (ebook) | LCC GV1469.35.M535 S48 2019 (print) |
    DDC 794.8—dc23

LC record available at https://lccn.loc.gov/2018012804

Manufactured in the United States of America
1-45067-35894-8/8/2018

CONTENTS

INTRODUCTION
BUILDING
DREAMS

**YOU'VE JUST ENTERED THE WORLD OF
MINECRAFT, AND YOU'RE PLAYING IN
SURVIVAL MODE.** The sky is growing dark.
Soon it will be night, and you'll have to defend
yourself against creepers, zombies, and spiders.
You have to build a shelter—fast.

Detailed buildings like these take a lot of materials and planning.

Luckily, you mined obsidian earlier. You also have wood and bricks in your **inventory**. Placing the building materials quickly, you build a small, rough shelter. Then you have a place to sleep and to store your belongings. You feel safe in your new home.

As you settle in to sleep for the night, you imagine the house you really want to construct. You'd like a more complex structure. You want it to be stronger, safer, and look more realistic. Ideas fill your head, and you think of the materials you'll need to find or craft when the sun rises. You want glass blocks for windows. You'd like some redstone that you can use to construct an automatic door. You want to create a lighting system for your house too.

You can't wait to get started on your next construction project.

Creepers appear in dark places and attack if you get too close.

A *Minecraft* inventory screen

CHAPTER 1
MATERIAL WORLD

MINECRAFT IS AN OPEN-WORLD GAME.
That means players can explore a vast landscape
and choose their own ways to play. Gamers have
nearly unlimited freedom to construct their own
virtual worlds. And what better way to get creative
than by building? Gamers have created all sorts of
incredible **structures** in _Minecraft_, basing them on
structures they've seen IRL (in real life), as well as
in their imaginations.

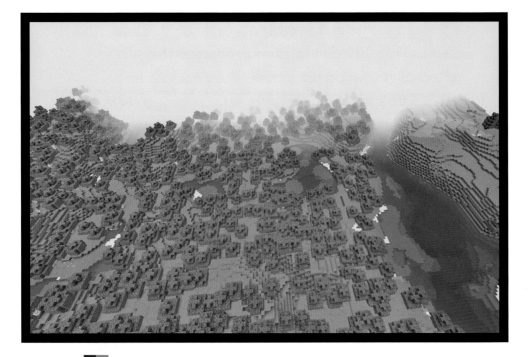

Minecraft's huge open world provides countless places to search for materials.

It starts with building materials. IRL, people use different materials to build different kinds of structures. You might use stone to build a house or wood to make a boat. That's true in *Minecraft*—except you can get even more creative with the types of materials you choose. You might still use wood to build a house. Or you could build a house using iron, stone, or even sponges.

You can choose many materials in *Minecraft*. Each material has different in-game **properties** that reflect its real-world properties. Water doesn't block a character's movement the way solid materials such as stone and clay do. Unlike stone, wool can burn. Some materials are **opaque**, such as sand and packed ice. Others are as **transparent** as clear glass.

Players need a variety of materials, such as bricks and glass, to build complex structures.

Minecraft is known for its blocky graphics, and many materials come in block shapes. But others are shaped more like the objects they represent. Plants look like flowers, carrots, wheat, and other shapes you'd recognize. These materials come in handy when you're constructing a garden. Fire in *Minecraft* looks like a flickering block that changes shape as if it were a moving flame.

Fire in *Minecraft* can spread to wood, grass, and other burnable materials.

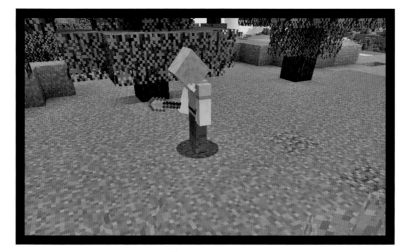

You can dig dirt with your bare hands, but it goes much faster with a shovel.

A huge variety of materials is available in *Minecraft*, but some are easier to obtain than others. You can harvest dirt from the top of the ground in many places. You can dig it up with your bare hands, but it goes much faster with a tool such as a shovel. Other materials, such as coal, have to be mined. You can find veins of coal ore in caves and cliff faces, and you need a pickax to mine it. Mining coal ore with a pickax produces one block of coal.

A pickax

Not everything about *Minecraft* reflects reality, though. Wood comes from trees, but gamers don't need an ax or any other special tool to get it. All you have to do is find a tree and choose the Chop command to obtain wood and add it to your inventory.

Once a material is in your inventory, you can use it on a building project by placing the material wherever you want it to go. There are lots of materials to try, and the construction options they offer are just about endless.

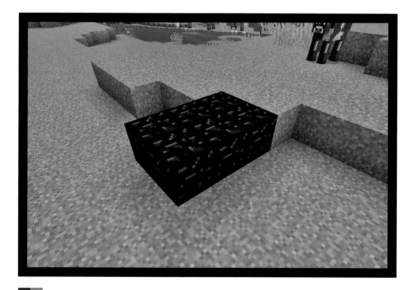

Obsidian is one of *Minecraft*'s strongest materials.

CHAPTER 2

HOME SWEET HOME

DO YOU WANT TO SURVIVE AND THRIVE IN *MINECRAFT*? If you're playing in Survival mode, you need a house to store your stuff and to sleep in at night. You'll have to take shelter from mobs—husks, creepers, zombies, and other enemies that are active at night.

You don't need a lot of materials to make a building like this one, and it can keep you safe at night.

It's up to you to choose the materials for your house. But it makes sense to select materials you'd use to build a house IRL, such as wood, brick, and cobblestone. After all, you want the building to be sturdy to keep out mobs and bad weather.

The smallest, easiest house you can build is the shape of a basic cube. It may not be that interesting to look at, but it's a safe option when you're in a hurry and don't have many materials.

STEMCRAFT

If you like designing your own buildings in *Minecraft*, consider yourself a digital architect. IRL, architects design structures with both form and function in mind. That means a building can look good while doing what it's supposed to do, such as providing shelter. Architects work on computers, similar to the way you design buildings in *Minecraft*. Architects use special software programs to design and draw their building plans.

Workers construct buildings based on detailed designs prepared by architects such as this one.

In Creative mode, gamers have unlimited building materials in their inventories from the start, and characters don't have to worry about surviving. This lets players focus on building complex structures that may have windows, stairs, and fun color patterns. You can even construct the kinds of buildings you see in your neighborhood.

A full inventory in Creative mode lets gamers get right to building.

Don't forget to raise the drawbridge before dusk!

But why limit yourself to what you see every day? *Minecraft* players can build fantastic structures too. You could make a castle with guard towers and **battlements** to guard against mobs. Or you could build a space needle, a building that extends up to a high point that offers excellent views plus protection against creepers.

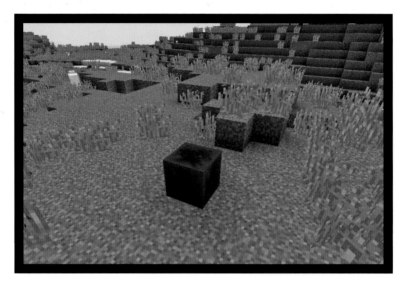

You can turn blocks of redstone like this one into redstone dust to power your creations.

Construction in *Minecraft* isn't limited to buildings. You can use the game's materials to make just about anything you want. Statues, famous **landmarks**, and high-tech vehicles are just a few of the things gamers have constructed. The things you build might look like realistic objects, or they might come from your imagination. It's even possible to create devices such as light switches, automatic doors, and musical instruments using redstone dust, a material that acts like electrical wiring in *Minecraft*.

CHAPTER 3
BIG CITY BUILDS

YOU'RE ROAMING THROUGH A CITY IN
MINECRAFT. You see parks, subway stations, churches, theaters, and skyscrapers. You come across some familiar sights: Times Square, Radio City Music Hall, and the Chrysler Building. The landmarks help you figure out exactly where you are. It's the *Minecraft* version of Manhattan in New York City!

It's fun to dream up your own ideas and construct them in *Minecraft*. Building a realistic city with *Minecraft* materials can be rewarding too, but it takes a lot of time and dedication. Gamers who do this pay careful attention to detail and use resources such as photos and maps for guidance.

Minecraft gamers can make sure their creations look realistic by comparing them to photos such as this image from Google Street View.

This photo of Monument Circle in Indianapolis has thousands of details that gamers can re-create in *Minecraft*.

Minecraft fan Eric Morrow and a friend consulted images from Google Street View and Apple Maps to construct downtown Indianapolis in the game. They built famous sites including Lucas Oil Stadium and Monument Circle. The project took them about eight months to complete. A video of their work has been viewed thousands of times on YouTube.

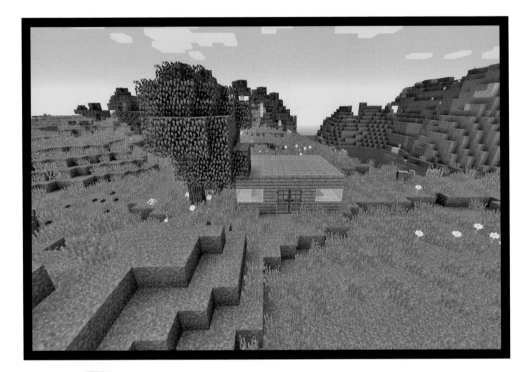

This building has a realistic size compared to the objects around it.

Like some other gamers who have built realistic cities in *Minecraft*, Morrow and his friend built their digital version of Indianapolis to **scale**. Building to scale means that the structures, streets, and other objects in a *Minecraft* city look realistic compared to one another. That way, a tree doesn't wind up larger than a skyscraper or smaller than a fire hydrant.

STEMCRAFT

Most designs, including *Minecraft* projects, can be scaled up to make them larger or scaled down to make them smaller. To scale down, you need to decide on a smaller measurement that will stand for a larger measurement. The friends who built Indianapolis in *Minecraft* decided that each digital block would represent a real-life block of a certain size. This helped them measure their *Minecraft* structures and compare them to structures IRL.

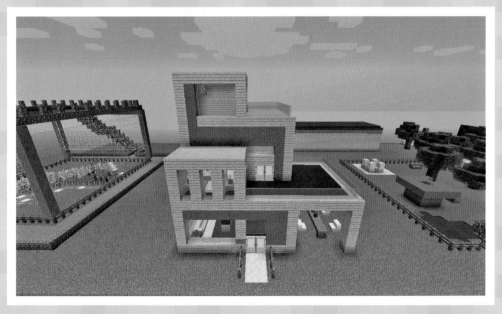

 Constructing a building block by block helps gamers control the size of their creations.

CHAPTER 4

WHAT'S NEXT?

MINECRAFT IS DIFFERENT FROM OTHER GAMES BECAUSE OF THE FREEDOM IT OFFERS PLAYERS. If you want to focus on exploring and fighting mobs, go for it. If you'd rather work on complex projects and achieve construction goals, you can do that too. And the game is always evolving to bring new excitement to players. So is the entire **brand**.

Will Arnett (*right*) interviews *Minecraft*'s lead creative designer, Jens Bergensten, at MineCon.

Just look at what's happening in the *Minecraft* world. In 2017 the brand's annual celebration, MineCon, went online as a live stream for the first time. Gamers from around the world could enjoy the show on their connected devices, no travel necessary. The fun show included several construction tutorials, advanced tips and secrets, and celebrities such as actor Will Arnett.

CODECRAFT

Suppose you're playing *Minecraft*, and you want to travel from a house you built to a faraway landmark. Sure, you could walk. But if you use a command, you could get there instantly. Players use commands to travel quickly, get items for their inventory, and even change time in the game.

Using commands in *Minecraft* is similar to writing computer code. To use commands, players type in the command bar on-screen. Each command starts with the forward slash (/) symbol. For example, typing "/time set day" into the command bar changes the game's time to day. Typing "/gamemode creative" switches the game from the mode you're playing to Creative mode. *Minecraft* has lots of commands that gamers can use to experiment.

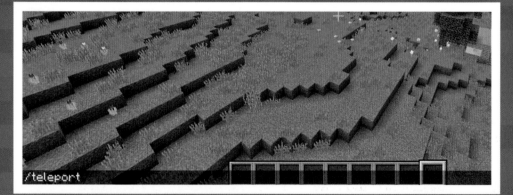

/teleport

The command bar appears as a black band at the bottom of the screen.

Fans got to view an early version of Update Aquatic at MineCon in 2017.

By the end of 2017, announcements about Update Aquatic started reaching gamers. This update to the *Minecraft* world promised fans oceans filled with sea creatures and shipwrecks to explore, as well as new underwater construction opportunities. In 2018 the people behind *Minecraft* released an update to the game so gamers could play together on different devices. That way, a player using a computer could play with a friend on a video game console.

In 2019 fans will flock to theaters to see the first *Minecraft* movie. The live-action film will be released in 3D and IMAX for people who really want to get into the action.

Expect more *Minecraft* updates and big announcements. Some players would like to see the game add features such as animal companions and new construction

A zombie (*left*) attacks a *Minecraft* character. Some gamers are hoping for new types of mobs in future updates.

Minecraft structures don't always have to serve a purpose. Sometimes they just look cool!

materials with unique properties. No matter what develops, construction will remain the creative heart of the game. Let your imagination run wild, and explore the endless building possibilities in *Minecraft*.

GLOSSARY

battlements: structures on walls that are used to defend buildings

brand: a group of products made by a company

inventory: resources such as building materials and tools that a character carries

landmarks: things that are easily seen and recognized from a distance

opaque: blocking light so objects on the other side cannot be seen

properties: qualities or features of something

scale: the size of something compared to something else

structures: things that are constructed

transparent: allowing light to pass through so objects can be seen on the other side

virtual: existing on a computer

FURTHER INFORMATION

ArchKIDecture
http://archkidecture.org/learn

Code.org
https://code.org/student

Jelley, Craig. Minecraft: *Guide to: Creative*. New York: Del Ray, 2017.

Martin, Chris. Minecraft: *The Business behind the Makers of Minecraft*. Minneapolis: Lerner Publications, 2016.

Minecraft Official Site
https://minecraft.net/en-us

Minecraft Wiki: Tutorials/Construction
https://minecraft.gamepedia.com/Tutorials/Construction

Needler, Matthew, and Phil Southam. Minecraft *Construction Handbook*. New York: Scholastic, 2015.

Schwartz, Heather E. *The World of* Minecraft. Minneapolis: Lerner Publications, 2018.

INDEX

PHOTO ACKNOWLEDGMENTS

Image credits: Various screenshots by Heather Schwartz; Matthias Ritzmann/Getty Images, p. 15; Google Street View screenshot, p. 20; Sean Pavone/Shutterstock.com, p. 21; Minecraft, *MINECON Earth 2017 Livestream* via YouTube, pp. 25, 27. Design element: COLCU/Shutterstock.com.

Cover: Minecraft screenshot/Egnez/Pixabay CC0.